# *HARMONIZATIOI*

# *TRANSPOSITION*

## *at the*

## *Keyboard*

**FOR THE STUDENT AND TEACHER OF**

**CLASS OR GROUP PIANO**

**PRIVATE PIANO**

**MUSIC EDUCATION**

**GENERAL EDUCATION**

### Alice M. Kern
UNIVERSITY OF MICHIGAN
### School of Music

© 1968, 1963 Summy-Birchard Music
division of Summy-Birchard Inc.
Exclusive print rights administered by Alfred Publishing Co., Inc.
All rights reserved. Printed in USA


ISBN 0-87487-059-3

**Summy-Birchard Inc.**
exclusively distributed by
Warner Bros. Publications Inc.
15800 N.W 48th Avenue
Miami, Florida 33014

# CONTENTS

# *INTRODUCTION*

STUDENTS OF PIANO whose major interest is in some field of music other than piano will use the piano as a tool in their chosen work; therefore, they will need to acquire specific skills in piano different from those of the student whose goal is concert performance.

For such students, one of these skills to be developed is the ability to harmonize at sight, in a free piano style, any given melody and to transpose it into other keys. The need for the development of this skill is being realized more and more, and it is now being required in the major universities and colleges, most particularly those institutions which have strong music education departments.

*Harmonization-Transposition at the Keyboard* has been written in answer to requests from university teachers of class piano and "functional piano." It has been conceived to meet the specific needs of those who must acquire the ability to harmonize melodies at sight.

For a number of years the author has worked with some two thousand students in piano classes of various levels of proficiency at the University of Michigan and has trained many teachers for class piano teaching. Through the years these teachers and students have asked for a book which, under one cover, would contain an abundance of material for harmonization, so that they would have at their disposal many melodies involving various harmonies, keys, and rhythms. For their use the author has assembled numerous melodies progressing from the simple to the more complex (adapting them where necessary), in each of several different categories.

This book is not intended to supplant a formal course in theory or keyboard harmony. Nor is it a book on improvisation or four-part harmony of any specific style. Its purpose is to present a simple method for harmonizing melodies in a free piano style suitable for use in public school work, folk dancing, community singing, rhythmic activities, etc. The method is one which can be understood by those who have a limited knowledge of keyboard harmony and lack experience in playing "by ear."

Part I is preparation for the actual harmonization, while Part II provides the melodies to be harmonized and transposed.

# *PREFACE*

MELODIES MAY BE harmonized in many different ways, depending on the training, musical taste, imagination, and the ear of the individual. The instructions in this book are addressed to the student who must rely on the harmonic structure of the melody rather than on his ear.

Chapter I is designed for the elementary piano student; therefore, only one position of the chords is suggested—the position employed in the majority of first-year piano books.

Chapter II, as well as succeeding chapters, offers a basic accompaniment figure in a free piano style which, when learned, enables the student to fix his eyes upon the melody which is being harmonized or transposed instead of watching his hands on the keyboard. It is necessary that Chapter II be thoroughly assimilated before attempting Chapter V, which introduces secondary triads.

The mastery of this practical approach to the rapid harmonization of a given melody will afford the basic knowledge and self-confidence necessary for imaginative improvisation. An awareness and exploration of various styles of accompaniment will further enhance this competence, provided there is constant endeavor.

The material in Part II has been graded in a way to insure ample practice on one specific problem before a new problem or harmony is introduced. Each chapter presents the simplest melodies first and progresses steadily to the more difficult. At the discretion of the teacher, the material need not be studied in the order in which it is given. Some teachers may wish to dwell upon the harmonization of minor melodies using tonic, subdominant, and dominant harmonies, while others may find it more beneficial to study secondary chords in major keys and altered chords before working in minor keys.

Proficiency in the use of the chords designated in each chapter should be secured before proceeding to another chapter.

The student should have ample drill on chords alone before attempting to harmonize the melodies. Also, students with little or no experience in transposition should be allowed to play the melody alone in many keys before attempting to harmonize while transposing. When the student has mastered the playing of chords with eyes closed and has acquired the ability to transpose the melody line, he should then be able to harmonize a melody in any key as easily as in the original key. Melodies in Chapter VIII and those in Chapter IX, section A, should be transposed into all major keys; those in Chapter X, section A, into all minor keys; the remainder of the melodies to be harmonized should be transposed to keys a minor 2nd, a major 2nd, a minor 3rd and a major 3rd above and below the original key.

ALICE KERN

# CHAPTER I

PREREQUISITES for chording melodies include the ability to sight-read with accuracy the simple melodies to be harmonized, a thorough knowledge of key signatures and intervals, and the ability to play major scales and three forms of the minor scale (natural, harmonic, and melodic) with hands separately at least one octave ascending and descending.

## Tonic and Dominant Seventh Harmonies

Triads are three-tone chords built in thirds. A major triad contains a root, a major third, and a perfect fifth. The dominant seventh, a four-tone chord, contains a major triad and the interval of a minor seventh.

The tonic (I) chord is built upon the first degree of the scale and includes the first, third, and fifth degrees. The dominant seventh (V⁷) chord is built upon the fifth degree of the scale and includes the fifth, seventh, second, and fourth degrees.

These chords may be inverted so that other members of the chord appear as the lowest tone. Examples 2 and 3 illustrate these chords in all inversions.

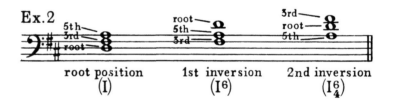

Omit the fifth of the V⁷ chord and practice the two chords as given in Example 4 in all keys.

Notice how simple it is to locate the V⁷ in this position and how the cadence may be played with eyes closed. The chord positions lie completely under the hand.

For chording all melodies in Chapter VIII in this book, only these two chords as shown in Example 4 are needed. Simple melodies may be chorded as follows, with one chord played on the first beat of each measure:

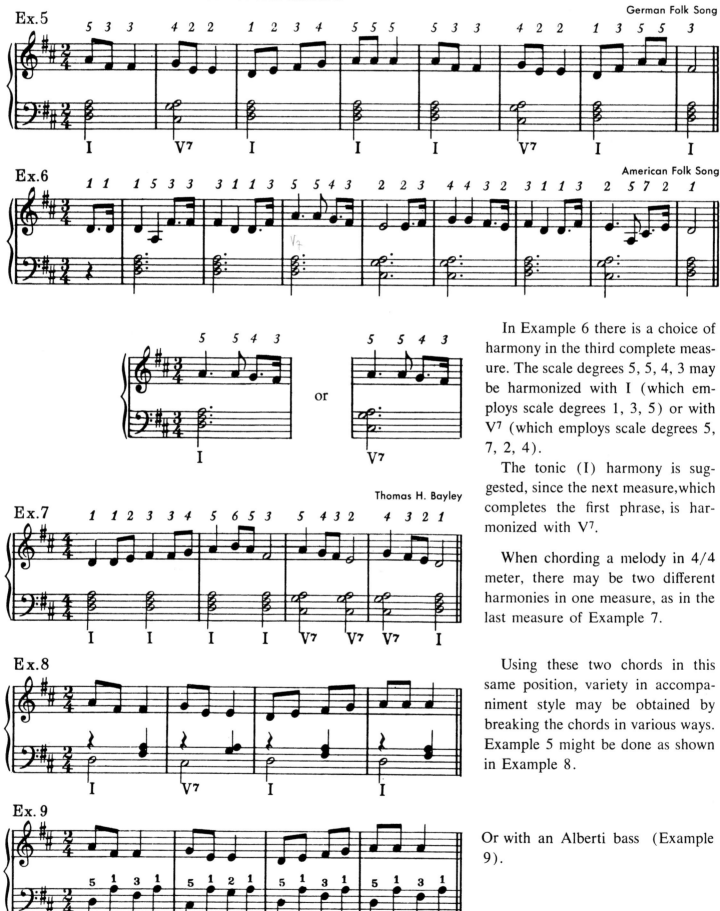

In Example 6 there is a choice of harmony in the third complete measure. The scale degrees 5, 5, 4, 3 may be harmonized with I (which employs scale degrees 1, 3, 5) or with $V^7$ (which employs scale degrees 5, 7, 2, 4).

The tonic (I) harmony is suggested, since the next measure, which completes the first phrase, is harmonized with $V^7$.

When chording a melody in 4/4 meter, there may be two different harmonies in one measure, as in the last measure of Example 7.

Using these two chords in this same position, variety in accompaniment style may be obtained by breaking the chords in various ways. Example 5 might be done as shown in Example 8.

Or with an Alberti bass (Example 9).

The same position of the two chords may be broken in the following ways for harmonizing Example 6:

**Ex. 10**

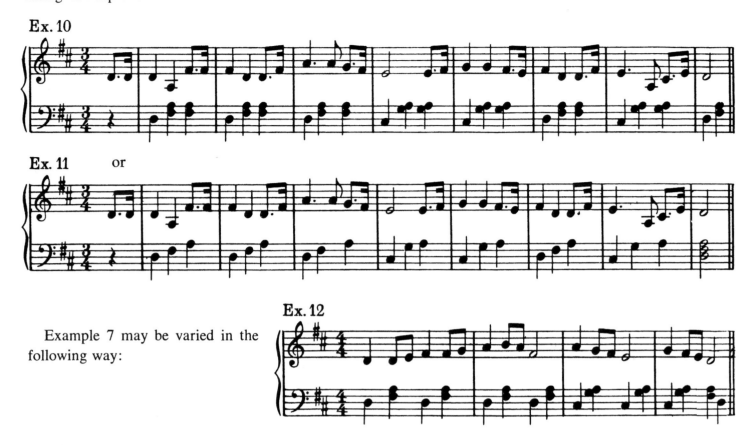

**Ex. 11**    or

Example 7 may be varied in the following way:

**Ex. 12**

## The Subdominant Chord  IV

With the addition of the subdominant chord you may now harmonize a multitude of familiar and unfamiliar melodies.

The subdominant chord is built upon the fourth degree of the scale and includes the fourth, sixth, and eighth (or first) scale degrees. Play it in its three positions.

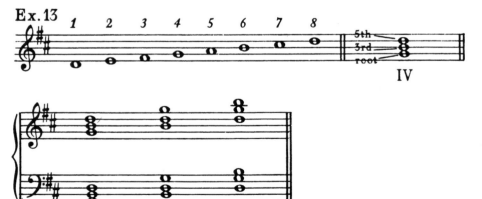

root position   1st inversion   2nd inversion

The position of the subdominant (IV) chord given in Example 14 is in its closest position to the tonic (I) chord. Practice the chords in Examples 14 and 15 with eyes closed and in all keys.

**Ex. 14**

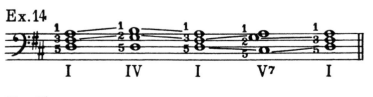

I    IV    I    V⁷    I

The same variations used in Examples 8, 9, 10, 11, and 12 may now be used to include the IV chord.

**Ex. 15**

I    IV    V⁷    I

All melodies given in Chapter IX can be harmonized with the three primary chords you have now learned. The following chart may help you in deciding which chords to use with the particular scale degree given in the melody:

| SCALE DEGREE | POSSIBLE CHORD |
|---|---|
| 1 | I, IV |
| 2 | $V^7$ |
| 3 | I |
| 4 | IV, $V^7$ |
| 5 | $V^7$, I |
| 6 | IV |
| 7 | $V^7$ |
| 8 | I, IV |

3/4 Meter: usually one chord to a measure
2/4 Meter: usually one chord to a measure
6/8 Meter: often two chords to a measure
4/4 Meter: usually two chords to a measure

Where there is a choice of chord, consider the remaining melody tones that will be played with the chord. If the fourth scale degree moves to the sixth scale degree, use a IV chord, since both the fourth and the sixth scale degrees belong to IV. If the fourth degree is moving down to the second, use $V^7$. If the first scale degree is moving to the fourth or sixth degrees, use IV, but if it is moving to the third or the fifth scale degrees, then use I.

## Harmonization in Minor Keys

Assuming that you have been playing minor scales in three forms as suggested at the beginning of the chapter, you realize that the tonic (I) chord, which is composed of the first, the third, and the fifth scale degrees, sounds different in minor keys because it contains a minor third rather than a major third between the root and the perfect fifth.

The chords you will use in harmonizing the melodies of Section A in Chapter X will be based upon the harmonic form of the minor scale. Limit yourself to these melodies in Section A until you have become quite proficient.

Since the seventh is raised in the harmonic form of the minor scale, it will be raised in the $V^7$ chord.

Here are the three principal chords in B minor given in the same positions as were the major chords. Again, we omit the fifth of $V^7$.

Practice these in all minor keys after reviewing each scale to make certain you have the key signature in mind. Listen to the minor I chord and most particularly to the minor IV.

**Ex.16** Harmonic form of B minor scale

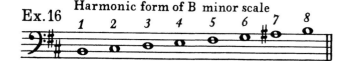

**Ex.17**

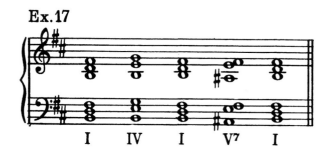

I   IV   I   $V^7$   I

# *CHAPTER II*

## I IV V in New Position

WHEN YOU HAVE BECOME proficient in deciding upon which harmonies to use and have learned to chord melodies as suggested in Chapter I, you are ready to use a different position of these same chords.

These three chords and their inversions were illustrated in Chapter I, Examples 2, 3, and 13. You have practiced these primary chords with the I in its root position followed by IV in its second inversion and V⁷ in its first inversion.

Once again omitting the fifth of V⁷, observe this same chord sequence in three different positions, noting that when a chord appears in its first inversion it is designated as I⁶ and in its second inversion as I⁶₄.

You are now ready to practice this chord sequence with I in its second inversion (Ex. 18c), adding the roots of the chords as bass tones to give breadth of motion. Include the fifth of V⁷ to make playing variations of the basic chord sequence easier.

To the above position of chords we add the root of the chord as an isolated bass tone.

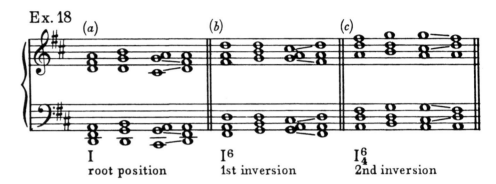

Ex. 18
(a) I — root position (b) I⁶ — 1st inversion (c) I⁶₄ — 2nd inversion

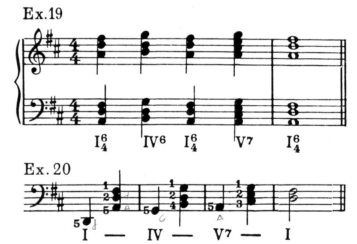

Ex.19
I⁶₄   IV⁶   I⁶₄   V⁷   I⁶₄

Ex. 20
I — IV — V⁷ — I

To skip from the bass note (root of the I chord) to the second inversion of the I chord will need practice until you are able to gauge the distance quickly. The remainder of the progression lies directly under the hand, enabling you to play it with eyes closed or with your eyes on the score of the melody which is to be harmonized. The playing of the chords in this position must become automatic.

Try Example 6, Chapter I with this accompaniment figure.

Ex. 21

I   I   I   V⁷   V⁷   I   V⁷   I

Observe how easy it is to *feel* the chords in the above accompaniment figure, how the chords lies directly under the hand; you need not even glance at the keyboard.

**Ex. 22**

*etc.*

Example 7 can also be harmonized with our new accompaniment figure.

**Ex. 23**

*etc.*

This same accompaniment can be varied in many ways: you may omit the bass note on the third beat;

**Ex. 24**

*etc.*

or you may break the triad.

**Ex. 25**

I    IV    V⁷    I

The three chords may also be broken in other ways.

I    IV    V⁷    I

I    IV    V⁷    I

A Latin American tune may call for a more characteristic rhythmic figure. Note that we still use our basic chord positions and eliminate watching the keyboard.

**Ex. 26**

I    IV    V⁷    I

# Chords in Right Hand

Rapid playing of chords in all positions is necessary before you attempt to fill in harmony under the melody in the right hand.

As a first step, try filling in the chord under the melody tone in the right hand on the main pulse beat of each measure where the left hand plays a single bass tone.

**Ex. 27**

Chords may also be filled in under the melody tone with the right hand and a single bass tone played with the left hand.

**Ex. 28**                                                      German Air

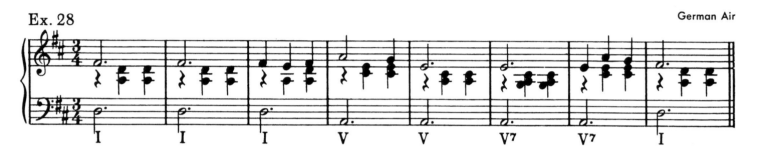

I   I   I   V   V   V⁷   V⁷   I

In the above illustrations the left hand plays the root of each chord as its lowest tone. When you are able to play the accompaniment figures shown thus far with fluency, you may use a different member of the chord as the bass note to give more variety.

**Ex. 29**

Example 28 was chorded with I for three consecutive measures. Use the fifth of I as the bass note in the second measure.

Notice the same style of accompaniment in the next melodies where the fifth of I is occasionally used as the bass tone.

**Ex. 30**                            Cornish Folk Dance

**Ex. 31**                                                      Scandinavian Folk Song

I   I⁶₄   I   V⁷   I   I⁶₄   V⁷   I

The same accompaniment figure you have been practicing may also be used in the harmonization of the melody of Example 31. Observe the second and sixth measures where you may play the fifth of I as the bass tone.

**Ex.32**

Other members of the IV and V[7] chords may also be used as the bass tone. Example 28 was chorded with V[7] in measures 4, 5, 6, and 7; try using the third of the chord as the bass tone in measure 5.

**Ex.33**

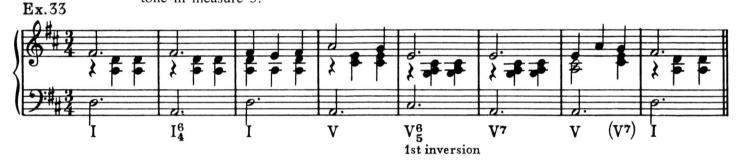

The following melody illustrates the use of the fifth of V[7] as the bass tone.

**Ex.34**                                                    Old English Air

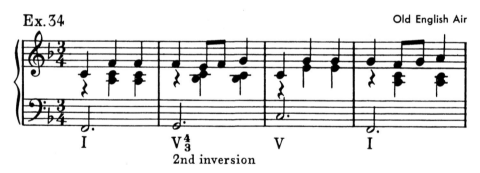

Example 35 illustrates the fifth of I and the third of V[7] as bass tones.

**Ex.35**                                                            A.M.K.

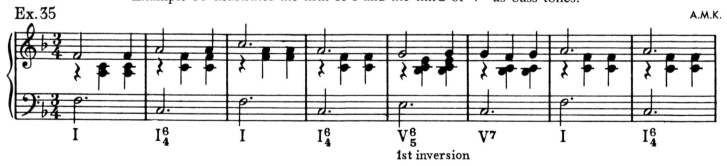

Now try playing a melody with the left hand and chords with the right.

**Ex.36**

# *CHAPTER III*

## Passing Tones and Changing Harmony within the Measure

PASSING TONES, or nonharmonic tones, may be defined as tones other than those belonging to the basic chord structure.

The first passing tones you will encounter will be unaccented passing tones, which are rhythmically weak. Examples may be found in Chapter VIII, No. 3, measure 7 and No. 5, measures 1, 2, 4, 5, and 7.

Melodies would be most uninteresting if all were to contain only the members of a chord; so it stands to reason that we must have passing tones for musical interest. Accented passing tones, which are nonharmonic tones appearing on the beat, delay the natural progression of a tone. Notice the accented passing tone appearing on the first beat of measure 4.

Up to this point you have found that a phrase usually ends with the tonic (I) or dominant (V) harmony. A phrase ending with V harmony gives a feeling of unrest as opposed to the feeling of repose derived from the I harmony; so a phrase ending with V will not occur at the end of a melody but at the halfway point. Therefore, notice that the accented passing tone occurring on the first beat of measure 4 in the above illustration is "pulling" toward the last note of the phrase, which is part of the dominant (V) chord.

Try the following melody, using two chords for each measure. The first beat of the last measure (the fourth scale degree) is a member of the IV chord and of the V chord, but to end the melody with either of these chords would impose a feeling of unrest; so you will treat this first tone of the last measure as an accented passing tone, chording the measure to fit the final tone, which is a member of the I chord.

Using one harmony for each measure (a general practice in 2/4 meter), chord Example 39. Take special note of measures 4 and 7, where the first beat of each will be treated as an accented passing tone or a nonharmonic tone.

In the next melody, using one harmony for each measure, you will find passing tones in the first three measures. The first scale degree appears most often in the first measure; so it would be chorded with I. The members of the I chord also appear most often in the second measure. Four notes in the third measure belong to the V⁷ chord.

In the majority of the melodies to be harmonized, the last chord will be I and the chord preceding it will be V.

## Changing Harmony within the Measure

Up to this point you have been using two harmonies for each measure when the melody is in 4/4 meter, and one harmony for each measure when the melody is in 2/4, 3/4, 3/8, or 6/8 meter.

Occasionally we have melodies which are greatly improved by adding an extra harmony. In 2/4 meter and 3/4 meter this will usually occur at a cadence point. A minuet is generally slower than a waltz, so the rhythmic flow is not disrupted by adding an additional harmony in a final cadence.

Notice the next to the last measure of the following minuet in which you will play a solid chord on the third beat.

**Ex. 41**                                                                 Mozart

Example 42, including only the last six measures of a melody, requires one harmony for the first half of the fifth measure as you would expect, but needs two harmonies for the

**Ex. 42**                                        Mozart

last half of the same measure. The majority of melody notes contained in that last half of the measure are members of I, but we need V for the final cadence; so you will play I for the third beat and $V^7$ for the fourth beat. Since it is the final cadence, you might use two block chords for the last two beats of the measure; or you might play the root of $V^7$ on count three, since it is also a member of the I chord and suggests a cadence of $I_4^6$, $V^7$, I. Try it both ways.

or

A melody in 6/8 meter very often requires two harmonies per measure. How many measures do you see in this next melody where two different harmonies are required?

**Ex. 43**                                                                Mozart

The first phrase will end with $V^7$ harmony; therefore the fourth measure could be chorded with I and $V^7$:

or played in the following way, since the root of $V^7$ is also the lowest tone of $I_4^6$.

Did you find the third measure should be chorded the same way? Did you chord the last measure with $V^7$ I?

# CHAPTER IV

## The Natural Minor

THE PRINCIPAL CHORDS as given in Chapter I will be adequate for chording the majority of minor melodies in this book.

In Chapter X, Section B, you will find melodies in the natural form of the minor scale. Before trying to chord these melodies in Chapter X, look through them carefully and notice the seventh scale degrees. If the seventh degree is not raised, it cannot be harmonized with $V^7$, since the $V^7$ chord contains a raised seventh. It may be harmonized in one of three ways, depending upon the harmonic structure of the melody and upon the mood of the melody:

1. It may be treated as an accented passing tone if the melody note following it is one scale step above or below it. When this is the case it is often harmonized with IV, as in the following illustrations.

Play I, IV, $V^7$ in E minor, then harmonize this melody.

Did you notice that the first note in the second measure—the lowered seventh—is treated as an accented passing tone progressing to a note which is a member of the IV chord? Example 45 in F minor is similar.

See whether you can find the lowered seventh in this folk tune in D minor and harmonize that particular measure with IV.

2. When the lowered seventh does not move in a stepwise fashion to the next scale degree above or below, but instead skips one or more degrees, this indicates a chord other than IV. Or, if the lowered seventh is repeated for a second beat, we can no longer treat it as an accented passing tone but must harmonize it with a chord which includes this particular note in its structure. In this case it might be harmonized with the major III, which is a major chord in a minor key.

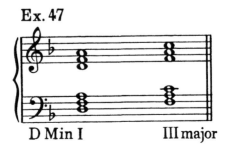

**Ex.48**

Welsh Folk Song

III major

Notice Example 48 in C minor where the lowered seventh (*b* flat) in measure 5 is repeated. It is approached and followed by an interval of a fourth.

You might harmonize the whole fifth measure with the major III, or you could use the major III for both the fifth and sixth measures; then again you might use the major III for measure 5 and for the first half of measure 6, chording the last half with I. Try each of the ways suggested.

The major III is also used where this major chord is suggested by the melody. In the following Spanish melody, notice the third measure: three of the five melody notes belong to the major III chord, indicating the use of this chord. If you should follow the first suggested harmonization and harmonize measure 3 with IV, the next measure, which requires IV, would lose its importance.

**Ex.49**

Spanish Folk Song

III major    IV

3. Another chord often used for harmonization of the lowered seventh is the minor triad built upon the fifth scale degree. Play I V⁷ in A minor, then play a minor triad on the fifth scale degree, which will be composed of a root, a minor third, and a perfect fifth. This chord is constructed from the natural form of the minor scale.

**Ex.50**

I — V minor 3rd

The following melody employs two of the members of the minor V in measure 4, and the complete chord in measures 10 and 14.

**Ex.51**

Irish Folk Song

V minor

V minor                    V minor

The next melody offers you a choice. The second measure contains a lowered seventh, which moves down a third to the next melody tone; therefore, you would not harmonize it with IV. The last two notes of the measure belong to the major III and also to the minor V, so either choice would be correct. Since this melody is to be played "Slowly and sadly," do you agree that the minor V might be more effective? Try it both ways.

You will have the same choice to make in the second measure of Example 53.

**Ex.52** *Slowly and sadly*

Irish Folk Song

G Minor         V minor

**Ex.53** *Plaintively*

Bohemian Folk Song

# CHAPTER V

## Secondary Triads in Major Keys

THE OCCASIONAL use of secondary triads will add color and interest to your harmonizations. One of the most useful of the secondary triads for this purpose is the supertonic (II) chord, which is built on the second degree of the scale and is composed of the second, fourth, and sixth scale degrees. It is a minor chord in a major key, since it contains a root, a minor third, and a perfect fifth. Play it in all positions.

**Ex. 54**

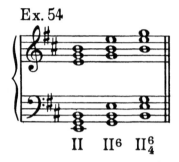

In the chord pattern we are using, we shall play the II in its first inversion (II⁶). Notice that only one tone of IV is changed to form the II⁶. With the third in the bass, it leads smoothly to V⁷ and is particularly effective when used to precede V⁷ at a cadence point.

**Ex. 55**

Play Example 56, using I and V⁷ harmonies first.

**Ex. 56**                                                                                              Provençal Carol

Now use II⁶ in the third measure and V⁷ in the fourth measure.

**Ex. 57**

A.M.K.

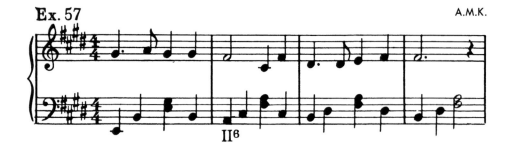

II⁶

In the first phrase of Example 57, II is clearly outlined,

**Ex. 58**

Old English Air

II⁶

also in Example 58.

Melodies to be harmonized including the use of II⁶ are found in Chapter XI, Section A.

Another secondary triad which you will find useful is the submediant (VI) chord, built on the sixth degree of the scale and composed of the sixth, first, and third scale degrees. Notice its similarity to the I chord. There are two tones common to both chords.

**Ex. 59**

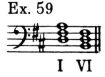

I  VI

The submediant (VI) is a minor chord in a major key. Its use will allow you more harmonic interest and will require more selectivity and discrimination.

In harmonizing each of the melodies in Chapter XI, Section B, you will find a place for the VI chord. The first melodies given will outline this new chord, but thereafter you will have to select carefully the place where you employ it.

**Ex. 60**

V⁷  I  V⁷  VI

Its use in a cadence as a substitute for I is effective when the cadence does not call for a feeling of repose. This type of cadence is called a Deceptive Cadence. Play the cadences in Example 60 and listen to the effect of each.

**Ex. 61**

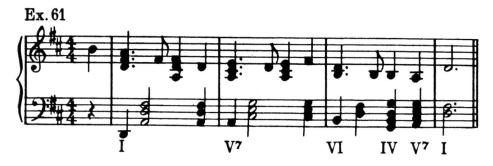

I          V⁷          VI  IV  V⁷  I

and in the last four measures of "Auld Lang Syne."

This VI chord often substitutes for the I to relieve the monotony of the repeated tonic (I) harmony. Notice its use in the third and fourth measures of "America,"

**Ex.62**

I  VI  IV  I⁶₄  VI

and in the following:

**Ex.63**

Beethoven

I  VI  II⁶  V⁷  I

In playing the chord pattern you have learned, add the VI chord after the I.

**Ex.64**

I — VI — IV — II⁶ — V⁷ — I

Now play Example 56, including the VI chord as a substitute for the I chord in the second measure, and listen to the difference in sound.

I  VI  II⁶  V⁷

The mediant (III) chord, a minor chord in a major key, will seldom be needed in the harmonization of the melodies in this book. In Chapter XI, Section C, you will find a few melodies where III may be used. Play the following, listening to the III chord:

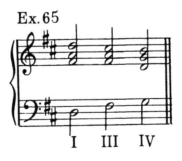

**Ex.65**

I  III  IV

We may now add secondary chords to the chart given in Chapter I.

| SCALE DEGREE | POSSIBLE CHORD |
|---|---|
| 1 | I, IV, VI |
| 2 | V⁷, II⁶ |
| 3 | I, VI, III |
| 4 | IV, V⁷, II⁶ |
| 5 | V⁷, I, III |
| 6 | IV, VI, II⁶ |
| 7 | V⁷, III |
| 8 | I, IV, VI |

# *CHAPTER VI*

## Secondary Dominants

YOU HAVE NOW learned to harmonize melodies using triads built upon all degrees of the scale with the exception of the seventh.

Ex.66

Each one of these triads, with the exception of VII, has its own dominant seventh. After playing the triads on I, II, III, IV, V, and VI, count up the interval of a fifth from the root of each to find the root of its dominant. Keeping in mind that all dominant seventh chords will sound alike because they are all composed of a root, a major third, a perfect fifth, and a minor seventh, try to find the dominant seventh of each of the six triads.

Ex.67

Ex.68

After playing Example 67 with right hand and then with left, try Example 68.

As added drill, build a dominant seventh chord ($V^7$) on every one of the twelve different keys, beginning with $c$ and moving chromatically to the next $c$.

Try it again and resolve each $V^7$ to its tonic (I) chord, first to major, then to minor.

## Dominant of the Dominant

Of the six secondary dominants given, you will find the dominant seventh of the dominant the most useful in chording the melodies in this book. It is built upon the second scale degree. The third of the chord is altered (raised), since a dominant seventh chord must contain a major third; therefore, it is often called an altered $II^7$. Henceforth it will be designated as $II^7_\#$.

Since II$^7_\sharp$ is the dominant seventh of V, it will usually be followed by V or V$^7$. In the music provided in this book the use of the II$^7_\sharp$ will usually occur at a cadence point where the phrase ends with dominant harmony.

Notice in Example 69 that the second phrase ends on a dominant harmony (V) and the preceding measure (measure 7) has a raised fourth, which is the altered member of the II$^7_\sharp$ chord.

Jessie L. Gaynor

Ex. 69

Example 70 is similar. Again you will find an altered fourth which points out the use of the new seventh chord.

Ex. 70 *Gaily*  British Folk Tune

Play these illustrations many times, transposing to several other keys, and listen to the color of this harmony so you are able to hear the chord quality implied in the next two examples where the altered fourth does not appear in the melody.

Ex. 71 *March*  Jessie L. Gaynor

✦ refers to raised 3rd

Ex. 72 *Allegretto*  British Folk Tune

The II$^7_\sharp$ is also used to add variety and color to a specific melody tone. Sing the chorus of "My Bonnie Lies Over the Ocean" and listen to the similarity of the two phrases. Because the first two measures of each of the two phrases are identical, it adds interest to harmonize them differently, making the repetition more distinctive. Play the two phrases, using the same harmonies for the first two measures of the *second* phrase that you used in the first two measures of the *first* phrase, then play as suggested.

Old English Air

Ex. 73

**Ex.74**

American Cowboy Song

Can you find a place to use II$_\sharp^7$ in "Home on the Range?"

**Ex.75**

I — VI — IV — II⁶ — V⁷ — I — II$_\sharp^7$ — V⁷ — I

♯ refers to raised 3rd

Play II$_\sharp^7$ in its root position to avoid confusing it with the II⁶ you have added to your chord sequence.

**Ex.76**

I — VI — II$_\sharp^7$ — V⁷ — I

♯ refers to raised 3rd

Also play the altered II⁷ after VI.

## Dominant of the Subdominant

In reviewing the secondary dominant seventh chords (Examples 67 and 68), observe that the root of the dominant of IV is also the root of I. A minor seventh is added to the I chord making it a I⁷♭; it resolves to IV.

**Ex.77**

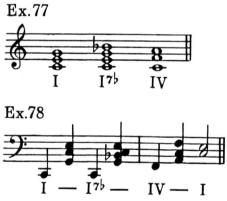

I  I⁷♭  IV

This I⁷♭ is most useful when tonic (I) harmony is repeated, then moves to IV.

**Ex.78**

I — I⁷♭ — IV — I

**Ex.79**

Irish Air

I  I⁷♭  IV —

Try "Believe Me, If All Those Endearing Young Charms," chording the first measure with I, then adding the minor seventh (*d* flat) to I as suggested.

**Ex.80**

I  III  IV  VI$_\sharp^7$  II⁶  V⁷  I

Other secondary dominants, V⁷ of II (VI⁷) and V⁷ of VI (III⁷) may be used in chording melodies in Chapters XII and XIII.

I  III$_\sharp^7$  VI

# *CHAPTER VII*

## Modulation

THE PROCESS OF changing key or tonality is called modulation. For chording the type of music presented in this book, we shall be concerned mainly with the following modulations:

> to the key of the dominant
> to the key of the subdominant
> from, a major key to its parallel minor
> from a major key to its relative minor
> from a minor key to its parallel major
> from a minor key to its relative major

These modulations may occur in any of the following ways:

1. A sudden change of key and establishment of that key at the beginning of a section, period, phrase, or sequential motive.
2. A gradual change of tonality by means of a chord progression.
3. As a "transitional" or "passing" modulation which leaves the new key almost as soon as it has been introduced.

These three types of modulation will be found in melodies of Chapter XIII and in some of the melodies in the succeeding chapters.

A study of the preceding chapter, and practice in the chording of melodies appearing in Chapter XII will make further explanation unnecessary for modulation to the key of the dominant or the subdominant. You have encountered many cadences to the key of the dominant; the only difference now is that, after reaching the key of the dominant via the use of II$^7_{\#}$, the melody will usually remain in the key of the dominant a little longer. The same will apply to modulation to the key of the subdominant (via I$^{7b}$).

In Example 81 written in the key of C, observe measure 6 chorded with V, measure 7 with II$^7_{\#}$ (or V$^7$ of the key of G), and the cadence ending on V. The second half of the melody, beginning after the double bar, remains in the key of the dominant (G) until the *f*-natural appears, which indicates a return to the original key of C by way of I$^{7b}$.

By using two different harmonies in measure 7 of the above example, the modulation to the new key would progress more smoothly. The VI chord of C major is the same as the II of the new key, G major. Therefore, the chording of the first two beats of the measure with VI and the last beat of the measure with $II_\sharp^7$ ($V^7$ of G), followed by I of G in measure 8, would imply a cadence of II $V^7$ I in G major.

**Ex. 82**

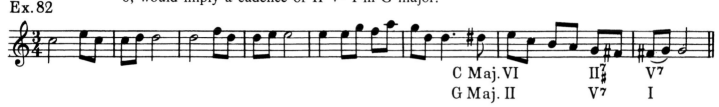

C Maj. VI       $II_\sharp^7$     $V^7$
G Maj. II       $V^7$      I

You have now modulated to the key of the dominant (from C to G) and then to the key of the subdominant (from G to C).

Modulating from a major key to its parallel minor (from C major to C minor), or from a minor key to its parallel major (from C minor to C major), is effected by the use of a pivot chord—one of the chords which the two keys have in common. The $V^7$ is common to both.

In modulating from a major key to its relative minor or from a minor key to its relative major, consider the chords they have in common.

**Ex. 83**   C Major                              A Minor

Any one of the chords which the two keys have in common may be played as a pivot chord to the relative key. If II in C major is the pivot chord, it becomes IV of the relative minor, and if IV in C major is the pivot chord, it becomes VI of the relative minor, etc.

**Ex. 84**   **Andante**                                         Spanish Folk Song

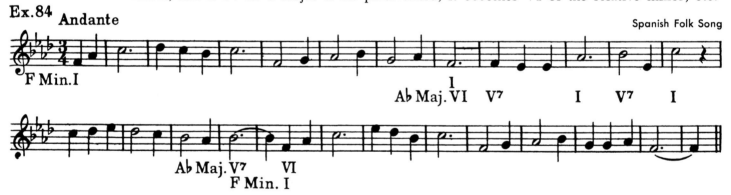

Since related keys have the same key signature (the I in minor being the same as VI in the relative major key), you will find many examples of melodies shifting very quickly from major to relative minor or from minor to relative major, as in the following:

**Ex. 85**                                                         Brahms

Modulations or "passing" modulations to keys other than those we have discussed will be encountered in a few of the melodies in Chapter XV. In such melodies, an accidental will show which of the secondary dominants may be used as part of the cadence to establish the new key.

# CHAPTER VIII
## Section A

## Section B

Ab

**Gently rocking** — Traditional

33

**Allegretto** — Greek

34

**Andante** — Neefe

35

**Allegretto** — British

36

**Allegro** — Mozart

37

**Andante** — Schubert

38

*p*

*p*

*rit.*

**Rather quick** — English

39

*f*

*f*

*mf*

# CHAPTER IX
## Section A

32

33

Pasukan berkuda

40

**Section B**

48

49

52

53

# CHAPTER X

## Section A

55

57

64

## Section B

70

*Minor triad on V

*III of G Minor (I of B♭ Major)

# CHAPTER XI
## Section A

76

78

## Section B

# Section C

# CHAPTER XII
## Section A

## Section B

## Section C

## Section D

# CHAPTER XIII

# CHAPTER XIV

118

120

# CHAPTER XV

122

126

128

# ACKNOWLEDGMENTS

Permission to draw material
from the following publications is gratefully acknowledged:

**THE AMERICAN SONGBAG**
compiled
by Carl Sandburg.
Copyright 1927 by
Harcourt, Brace
and Company, Inc.

Melodies No. 28, 61, 72, 76, 88, 93, 111, 115, 153, 311, 324, 340, 362, 502.

**CHRISTMAS CAROLS FROM MANY COUNTRIES**
arranged by
Satis N. Coleman
and Elin K. Jorgensen.
Copyright 1934 by
G. Schirmer, Inc.

Melodies No. 11, 97, 238.

**FOLK-DANCE MUSIC**
by Elizabeth Burchenal
and C. Ward Crampton.
Copyright 1908, 1936
by G. Schirmer, Inc.

Melodies No. 2, 30, 67, 74, 87, 90, 144, 161, 180, 208, 288, 338, 473.

**MARCH AND DANCE ALBUM**
by Arthur Somervell.
Copyright 1909 by
Boosey & Co.

Melodies No. 12, 109, 132, 155, 162, 279, 347, 412, 445, 492, 494, 509, 511, 524, 541.

**THE NEW NATIONAL SONG BOOK**
edited by
Sydney Northcote
and Herbert Wiseman.
Copyright 1958 by
Boosey and Hawkes, Inc.

Melodies No. 24, 39, 104, 112, 117, 123, 126, 137, 152, 158, 164, 165, 199, 209, 247, 266, 267, 272, 275, 281, 304, 327, 331, 332, 341, 343, 353, 366, 371, 376, 378, 379, 380, 384, 387, 396, 409, 414, 416, 419, 429, 443, 456, 461, 490, 491, 498, 499, 511, 529, 540.

**NATIONAL SONGS OF WALES**
edited by E. T. Davies
and Sydney Northcote.
Copyright 1959 by
Boosey and Hawkes, Inc.

Melodies No. 21, 68, 71, 75, 84, 89, 121, 182, 189, 211, 215, 218, 219, 220, 236, 243, 277, 297, 330, 339, 365, 370, 383, 385, 386, 397, 398, 406, 436, 440, 455, 520, 540, 543, 549.